Apr 18

THE
Instant Pot®
COOKBOOK

DEVELOPED BY

WILLIAMS SONOMA

TEST KITCHEN

Photographs John Lee

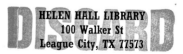
weldon**owen**

CONTENTS

Blueberry-Pecan Cheesecake (page 50)

Spiced Carrot & Cashew Soup (page 17)

IN PRAISE OF THE INSTANT POT®

When it comes to the newest craze in kitchen gadgetry, the Instant Pot® has serious staying power. Since the multifaceted countertop kitchen appliance first debuted in 2009, it has garnered hundreds of thousands of fans who enthusiastically applaud its ability to cut cooking time, transform tough cuts of meat to tender perfection, cook recipe staples like beans and rice in large quantities, and self-regulate a slew of safety features. Its many ardent admirers profess that once you begin to understand the Instant Pot's most basic functions, you can retire your slow cooker, pressure cooker, rice cooker, and yogurt maker because it accomplishes all those tasks and more—freeing up a lot of countertop real estate in the process.

The Instant Pot® can sear, sauté, steam, pressure cook, and slow roast all in one pot, and in hours less than it would take to cook conventionally. A whole chicken cooks in 25 minutes, paella in under 15 minutes, chili in 30 minutes, and risotto in 10 minutes without the usual requirement of constant stirring. Arguably best in the Instant Pot® are large chunks of meat—like pork shoulder and beef chuck—that cook up every bit as deliciously as in a slow cooker, just a day or two faster. There are also the sleeper hits of the Instant Pot®—surprising successes like hard-cooked eggs (page 28) and cheesecake (page 51)—that utilize the pot's special attributes to cook perfectly.

The Instant Pot® is as big on flavor as it is short on time. The moment the lid is locked in place and the cooking begins, all the vitamins, minerals, and heady aromas are trapped in the pot, where they remain until serving, guaranteeing more healthful, flavorful, and satisfying meals. Soups, such as chunky vegetable chowder (page 23) and spiced carrot purée (page 17), take on all the nuances of the ingredients and seasonings with which they are cooked. Classic dishes such as chicken posole (page 27), coq au vin (page 41), and chili (page 20) build to an easy flavor infusion once only achievable from long, slow cooking. With the following recipes and some knowledge of the Instant Pot's basic functions, countertop cooking will become your favorite way to put a meal on the table.

COOKING WITH AN INSTANT POT®

The Instant Pot® is available in different models and sizes. Each has slightly varying attributes, but all accomplish the same basic functions.

All of the Instant Pot® models have the following cooking program keys, aka function keys: Manual (on older pots) or Pressure Cook (on newer pots), Soup/Broth, Meat/Stew, Bean/Chili, Slow Cook, Sauté, Rice, Multigrain, Porridge, and Steam. All but one model has a Poultry program; Yogurt is available on most models; and Cake, Egg, and Sterilize programs are on only select models.

In this book, the two most commonly used program keys are Manual/Pressure Cook, which is equivalent to cooking in a pressure cooker, and Sauté, a non-pressure setting that allows you to sauté, brown, and simmer foods in the uncovered pot. The names on the other keys reflect their primary uses, such as Soup/Broth for preparing everything from thick chowders to clear stocks, Rice for cooking any type of white rice, and Meat/Stew for protein-rich braises. Slow Cook and Yogurt, like Sauté, are non-pressure settings.

The operation keys are used to adjust the pressure and the cook time for pressure cooking programs. On most models, the Pressure button switches between Low and High pressure and the Adjust button between Less, Normal, and More cook time (the default time for each setting appears in the lighted display). The - and + buttons are used to override any default cook time when needed. The Adjust button is also used to select the heat level (Less, Normal, and More) for non-pressure programs.

The LCD display on the panel shows how much time remains on the selected program and whether the pot is off or on. The Keep Warm/Cancel button ends any cooking program, automatically switching the pot to the Keep Warm setting. On the lid is the Pressure Release handle, which is called Steam Release on some models and is referred to as "the valve" in the recipes in this book. It moves between Sealing, for bringing up pressure, and Venting, for releasing pressure.

Once you become accustomed to cooking with the Instant Pot®, the specialized functions will become inuitive. As with most new appliances, the best way to master the Instant Pot® is simply to use it.

THE MODELS

The Instant Pot® is currently available in three basic models, the Lux, Duo, Duo Plus, and Ultra. The numbers in the model names, 60 and 80, refer to the size of the pot, 6 and 8 quarts respectively. Each has slightly different cooking features, with up to fifteen different cooking programs to choose from, depending on the model. The recipes in this book were developed in the Williams Sonoma Test Kitchen using the Duo Plus 6Qt Instant Pot®.

INSTANT POT® PRIMER

The Instant Pot® is most commonly used for cooking foods under pressure. Refer to your pot's manual for details on specialized cooking programs and model-specific instructions.

Using the Pressure Cooking Programs

Instant Pot® pressure cooking starts with these basic steps:

1 Always add at least 2 cups liquid to the pot when cooking under pressure. Any less and not enough steam will be generated.

2 Put the food to be cooked in the pot, being careful not to fill it more than two-thirds full.

3 Cover the pot with the lid, lock the lid in place, and move the Steam Release handle (the valve) to Sealing.

4 Press the button for the desired cooking program. A preset time (Normal) will appear in the lighted display. You now have 10 seconds to alter the time, selecting either Less or More or using the - and + keys, or to change the pressure, using the Pressure button.

5 Once the 10 seconds have elapsed, the pot will beep and the lighted display will indicate the cycle has started. When the cycle has finished, the pot will beep again and automatically end cooking.

6 Release the pressure using the natural-release or quick-release method, then press Keep Warm/Cancel. When the LCD display goes off, open the lid.

HIGH ALTITUDE COOKING

If you are cooking at 3,000 feet and are using the pressure cooking programs on your Instant Pot®, you will need to increase the cook times by 5 percent. For every 1,000 feet above 3,000, increase the cook times by an additional 5 percent, so that cook times would increase by 10 percent at 4,000 feet, 15 percent at 5,000 feet, and so on.

Pork & Green Chile Tamales (page 44)

Using the Sauté Program

The Sauté program is the most frequently used non-pressure program. To use the sauté mode, follow these basic steps:

1 With the pot empty and uncovered, press the Sauté button, then use the Adjust/Sauté button to adjust the temperature.

2 When the LCD display reads Hot, add the oil, butter, or food and sauté, brown, or sear as needed, then continue as directed in individual recipes.

Other Features

Once you've mastered the basic functions, a few key steps will finish the cooking cycle.

Delay Start: This feature allows you to delay the start of cooking. It is particularly handy for soaking beans before cooking them.

Keep Warm/Cancel: This button turns off any cooking program, allowing you to switch to another program, such as from Sauté to Soup/Broth, or to end cooking. It also starts up the Keep Warm setting, which will keep the food at a safe temperature for up to 10 hours.

Pressure Release: Each recipe specifies either a natural release of steam (for heartier foods that benefit from additional cooking by residual steam) or a quick release (for delicate, quicker-cooking foods). For the natural release, once the cooking program ends, let the pressure diminish on its own, which can take from a few minutes to more than a half hour. For the quick release, move the Pressure Release handle on the lid to Venting to release the steam. Once the steam has stopped and the float valve has dropped, press Keep Warm/Cancel and open the lid. You can also combine the methods by letting the steam release naturally for 10 minutes or so, followed by a quick release.

TIPS & TROUBLESHOOTING

• *Never fill the pot more than two-thirds full to allow enough room for steam to build, or more than half full if cooking rice or beans to give them room to expand.*

• *When using the Steam program, always use the steam rack that came with the pot (or any metal or silicone trivet or basket). The pot comes to pressure on full, continuous heat, and the food can scorch if not raised off the pot bottom.*

• *Cook time starts from when the pot reaches full pressure, not from moment at which the program button was pressed. Building up pressure and releasing pressure can take from a few minutes to 30 minutes or more, depending on the amount of food, the temperature, and the release method.*

• *When switching between cooking programs, always press the Keep Warm/Cancel button to stop the current function before selecting a new one.*

THAI CHICKEN NOODLE BOWLS

Begin marinating the chicken the night before you plan to serve this easy meal-in-a-bowl and it will be on the dinner table in minutes. The richly flavored sauce does double duty as chicken marinade and noodle seasoning.

In a bowl, whisk together the vinegar, sesame oil, peanut butter, soy sauce, fish sauce, lime juice, sugar, chile paste, and ginger to make a sauce. In a second bowl, combine the chicken and ¼ cup of the sauce and turn to coat. Cover and marinate at room temperature for at least 20 minutes or in the refrigerator for up to overnight.

Select Sauté More on the Instant Pot® and warm the canola oil. In batches, sear the chicken until browned on both sides, about 3 minutes per side. Add the remaining sauce to the pot and stir well.

Lock the lid in place and turn the valve to Sealing. Press the Keep Warm/Cancel button to reset the program, then press the Manual/Pressure Cook button and set the cook time for 8 minutes at high pressure.

Meanwhile, cook the rice noodles according to the package instructions, then drain, reserving ¼ cup of the cooking water.

When the cooking is complete, turn the valve to Venting to manually release the steam. When the steam stops, carefully remove the lid and transfer the chicken to a large bowl. Use 2 forks to shred the chicken into bite-size pieces. Add the rice noodles to the pot and toss with the sauce, adding the reserved cooking water as needed to achieve the desired consistency.

Divide the noodles evenly among individual bowls and top with the chicken and garnishes of choice.

SERVES 4

½ cup rice vinegar

½ cup Asian sesame oil

¼ cup creamy peanut butter

3 tablespoons soy sauce

2 tablespoons fish sauce

2 tablespoons fresh lime juice

1 tablespoon firmly packed golden brown sugar

2 teaspoons roasted red chile paste

1 tablespoon peeled and grated fresh ginger

1 lb boneless, skinless chicken thighs

1 tablespoon canola oil

½ lb dried rice noodles

GARNISH OPTIONS

bean sprouts

micro greens

dry-roasted peanuts

sliced green onions

sliced jalapeño chile

julienned fresh basil

julienned carrots

lime wedges

Pump up the vegetables by adding baby spinach or kale leaves, or add any of your own favorite noodle bowl garnishes.

For a hit of extra heat
and a splash of color,
sprinkle soup bowls
with a last-minute
dash of chili powder
or smoked paprika just
before serving.

SPICED CARROT & CASHEW SOUP

Smooth and creamy, this appealing soup draws on the Indian pantry for much of its lively aroma and flavor. Moderately spicy Madras curry powder is a good choice here, but use whatever type suits your palate.

Select Sauté on the Instant Pot® and warm the oil. Add the carrots, celery, and onion and cook, stirring occasionally, until the vegetables begin to brown, about 5 minutes. Add the garlic, curry powder, paprika, cumin, chili powder, ginger, and cayenne, season with salt and pepper, and continue to cook, stirring occasionally, until the vegetables are well coated with the spices, about 5 minutes more. Add the cashews, bay leaf, and broth and stir to combine.

Lock the lid in place and turn the valve to Sealing. Press the Keep Warm/Cancel button to reset the program, then press the Soup button and set the cook time for 20 minutes at high pressure.

Turn the valve to Venting to manually release the steam. When the steam stops, carefully remove the lid and transfer half of the mixture to a blender. Process the soup on high speed until smooth and creamy. Transfer the purée to a saucepan, process the remaining half the same way, and add to the saucepan.

Heat the soup on the stove top over medium-hot heat until piping hot. Stir in the orange zest. Taste and adjust the seasoning with salt and black pepper. Divide among individual bowls, garnish with crème fraîche, tarragon, and almonds, and serve.

SERVES 6

3 tablespoons olive oil

6 carrots, peeled and chopped

2 ribs celery, chopped

1 yellow onion, chopped

2 cloves garlic, minced

2 teaspoons curry powder

1 teaspoon smoked paprika

¾ teaspoon ground cumin

½ teaspoon chili powder

½ teaspoon ground ginger

Pinch of cayenne pepper

Salt and freshly ground black pepper

2 cups raw, unsalted cashews

1 bay leaf

4 cups chicken or vegetable broth

2 teaspoons grated orange zest

Crème fraîche, fresh tarragon leaves, and chopped toasted almonds, for garnish

ORANGE-CHILE CHICKEN LETTUCE WRAPS

The Instant Pot® shows off its versatility in this version of spicy chicken lettuce wraps, acting first as a sauté pan, then as a pressure cooker, and then again as a sauté pan for thickening the sauce.

In a bowl, toss the chicken with 2 tablespoons of the cornstarch to coat evenly. Select Sauté on the Instant Pot® and warm the canola oil. In batches, cook the chicken, turning as needed, until golden brown on all sides, about 6 minutes. Add the water, soy sauce, sugar, vinegar, sesame oil, chile-garlic sauce, and ½ cup of the orange juice and stir to mix well.

Lock the lid in place and turn the valve to Sealing. Press the Keep Warm/Cancel button to reset the program, then press the Poultry button and set the cook time for 7 minutes at high pressure.

Let the steam release naturally for about 10 minutes, then turn the valve to Venting to release any residual steam. Carefully remove the lid and transfer about ¼ cup of the sauce to a small bowl. Add the remaining 3 tablespoons cornstarch to the bowl and stir to dissolve. Return the mixture to the pot and stir well. Press the Keep Warm/Cancel button to reset the program, then press the Sauté button and cook, stirring occasionally, until the sauce thickens, about 5 minutes. Stir in the remaining ½ cup orange juice and the orange zest and season with salt and pepper.

Arrange the lettuce leaves on a large serving platter and scoop the chicken into them. Top with your choice of garnishes and serve.

SERVES 4

2 lb boneless, skinless chicken breasts, cut into 2-inch cubes

5 tablespoons cornstarch

2 tablespoons canola oil

⅓ cup water

¼ cup soy sauce

2 tablespoons firmly packed golden brown sugar

1 tablespoon rice vinegar

1 tablespoon Asian sesame oil

1 teaspoon chile-garlic sauce

1 cup fresh orange juice

1 tablespoon grated orange zest

Kosher salt and freshly ground pepper

1 or 2 small heads Bibb, butter, or baby romaine lettuce leaves, for serving

Sliced cucumbers, radishes, and green onions, julienned carrot, and red pepper flakes, for garnish

Serve the lettuce leaves, chicken, and garnishes at the table and encourage everyone to add their own favorite ingredients.

RED BEAN CHILI WITH ANDOUILLE

If you cannot find andouille, a spiced and smoked pork sausage prized by Cajun cooks, kielbasa or another smoked sausage can be substituted. You can also trade out the kidney beans for cannellini or pinto beans, if you like.

Pick over the beans, discarding any grit or misshapen beans, then rinse, place in a bowl with water to cover, and let soak for at least 8 hours or up to overnight.

Select Sauté on the Instant Pot® and warm the oil. Add the sausage and cook, stirring occasionally, until browned, about 4 minutes. Using a slotted spoon, transfer the sausage to a plate. Add the ground beef to the pot, season with salt and pepper, and cook, stirring to breaking up the meat with a wooden spoon, until browned, about 4 minutes. Using the slotted spoon, transfer the beef to the plate with the sausage. Add the onion to the pot and cook, stirring occasionally, until beginning to soften, about 2 minutes. Add the bell pepper, celery, and garlic and cook, continuing to stir, until softened, about 3 minutes. Stir in the chili powder, cumin, paprika, and 1 teaspoon salt, mixing well. Drain the beans and add to the pot along with the cooked sausage and beef, the diced and crushed tomatoes, and the water.

Lock the lid in place and turn the valve to Sealing. Press the Keep Warm/Cancel button to reset the program, then press the Bean/Chili button and set the cook time for 30 minutes.

Turn the valve to Venting to manually release the steam. When the steam stops, carefully remove the lid and stir in the green onions and season with salt and pepper.

If using rice, spoon it into bowls, then ladle the chili over the top and serve.

SERVES 6

1 cup dried red kidney beans

1 tablespoon olive oil

¾ lb andouille sausage, halved lengthwise then cut crosswise into ½-inch-thick pieces

1 lb ground beef

Kosher salt and freshly ground pepper

1 yellow onion, diced

1 green bell pepper, seeded and diced

1 rib celery, diced

4 cloves garlic, minced

2 tablespoons chili powder

1 tablespoon ground cumin

1 teaspoon smoked paprika

1 can (10 oz) Mexican-style diced tomatoes with juice

1 can (14½ oz) crushed tomatoes with juice

2 cups water

4 green onions, thinly sliced

Cooked long-grain white rice (page 53), for serving (optional)

LEEK & GOAT CHEESE STRATA

A strata is usually layered, but for this Instant Pot® version, the eggs, cheese, and bread are stirred together with delicious results. You can toast the bread a day in advance; store it in an airtight container.

Preheat the oven to 350°F. On a sheet pan, toss the bread cubes with the oil, coating evenly. Season with salt and spread in a single layer. Bake until golden and crisp, about 15 minutes.

Select Sauté on the Instant Pot® and melt the butter. Add the leek and a pinch of salt and cook, stirring occasionally, until softened, about 5 minutes. Add the chives and tarragon and cook, stirring occasionally, until fragrant, about 30 seconds. Transfer the leeks to a bowl and let cool slightly.

Using pot holders, lift out the inner pot and wipe it out or rinse and dry it. Coat the bottom and lower sides of the pot evenly with cooking spray and return it to the Instant Pot® housing. In a large bowl, whisk together the eggs, milk, cheese, 1 teaspoon salt, and the pepper. Add the toasted bread, leek mixture, and goat cheese, stir to combine, and pour into the Instant Pot.® Lock the lid in place and turn the valve to Sealing. Press the Manual/Pressure Cook button and set the cook time for 10 minutes on high pressure.

Let the steam release naturally for 5 minutes, then turn the valve to Venting to release any residual steam. Carefully remove the lid, spoon the strata onto individual plates, and serve.

SERVES 4–6

½ lb French bread, cut into 1-inch cubes

1 tablespoon olive oil

Salt and freshly ground pepper

2 tablespoons unsalted butter

1 large leek, about 10 oz, halved and thinly sliced crosswise

2 tablespoons minced fresh chives

1 teaspoon minced fresh tarragon

Cooking spray

8 large eggs

¾ cup whole milk

¼ cup grated Parmesan cheese

¼ teaspoon freshly ground pepper

¼ lb fresh goat cheese, crumbled

For a vegetarian chowder, omit the bacon and cook the onion in 2 tablespoons unsalted butter instead of the bacon fat.

SUMMER CORN & ZUCCHINI CHOWDER

This hearty chowder draws on two of summertime's favorite garden harvests. If you like, substitute yellow straight-neck or green-striped Costata Romanesco squash for the zucchini.

Select Sauté on the Instant Pot® and warm the oil. Add the zucchini, green onions, and thyme and cook, stirring occasionally, until the zucchini are tender, about 5 minutes. Season with salt and pepper. Transfer the zucchini to a bowl.

Switch to Sauté More, add the bacon, and cook, stirring occasionally, until crisp, about 5 minutes. Transfer the bacon to a plate. Spoon out all but 1 tablespoon of the fat from the pot and discard. Add the onion to the pot and cook, stirring often, until tender, about 3 minutes. Add the garlic and cook, stirring, for 30 seconds. Add the corncobs, bay, thyme, and water.

Lock the lid in place and turn the valve to Sealing. Press the Keep Warm/Cancel button to reset the program, then press the Manual/Pressure Cook button and set the cook time for 10 minutes at high pressure.

Turn the valve to Venting to manually release the steam, then carefully remove the lid. Discard the corncobs. Add the potatoes, corn kernels, and half of the bacon and season with salt and pepper. Lock the lid in place and turn the valve to Sealing. Press the Keep Warm/Cancel button to reset the program, then press the Manual/Pressure Cook button and set the cook time for 4 minutes at high pressure.

Turn the valve to Venting to manually release the steam, then carefully remove the lid. Press the Keep Warm/Cancel button to reset the program, then select Sauté, stir in the cream, milk, cayenne, and zucchini, and heat until hot.

Ladle into individual bowls, garnish with the chives and remaining bacon, season with salt and pepper, and serve.

1 tablespoon olive oil

2 zucchini, thinly sliced

2 green onions, thinly sliced

1 teaspoon fresh thyme leaves

Kosher salt and freshly ground black pepper

½ lb sliced bacon, diced

1 yellow onion, diced

2 cloves garlic, minced

Kernels from 6 ears corn, cobs reserved

1 bay leaf

2 fresh thyme sprigs

2½ cups water

4 red potatoes, cut into ½-inch dice

1 cup heavy cream

1 cup whole milk

¼ teaspoon cayenne pepper

3 tablespoons minced fresh chives

SERVES 4

WALDORF CHICKEN SALAD

Named for New York's Waldorf-Astoria Hotel, the Waldorf salad traditionally included only apples and celery bound by mayonnaise. Here, perfectly tender chicken adds to the classic mix.

To cook the chicken, put the onion, carrots, celery, garlic, and water in the Instant Pot, then place the steam rack on the pot bottom. Season the chicken inside and out with the salt and pepper and place it, breast side up, on the rack. Lock the lid in place and turn the valve to Sealing. Press the Manual/Pressure Cook button and set the cook time for 25 minutes at high pressure.

Let the steam release naturally for 20 minutes, then turn the valve to Venting to release any residual steam. Carefully remove the lid and transfer the chicken to a cutting board. When cool enough to handle, remove the meat, discarding the skin and bones. Cut enough meat into 1-inch cubes to measure 2 cups for the salad. Reserve the remaining meat for another use.

To make the salad, in a large bowl, whisk together the mayonnaise, yogurt, and lemon juice. Season with salt and pepper. Add the apple, grapes, celery, fennel, cashews, and cubed chicken and toss to coat evenly. Taste and adjust the seasoning with salt and pepper.

Arrange a bed of endive leaves on a serving platter and top with the salad. Garnish with fennel fronds and serve.

SERVES 6

FOR THE CHICKEN

1 yellow onion, quartered

2 carrots, peeled and cut into 2-inch lengths

2 ribs celery, cut into 2-inch segments

4 cloves garlic, smashed

2 cups water

1 whole chicken, 4 lb

1 tablespoon kosher salt

½ tsp ground pepper

FOR THE SALAD

½ cup mayonnaise

2 tablespoons plain Greek yogurt

1 tablespoon fresh lemon juice

Kosher salt and freshly ground pepper

1 cup diced apple

1 cup seedless red grapes, halved

½ cup finely diced celery

½ cup thinly sliced fennel, plus fennel fronds for garnish

¾ cup salted roasted cashews

1–2 heads Belgian endive, leaves separated

Offer this chunky salad in appetizer portions (as here), or spoon it into butter lettuce cups for larger servings.

For variety at the table, expand the choice of garnishes by offering small bowls of thinly sliced jalapeño, radishes, and green onion.

CHICKEN POSOLE WITH TOMATILLOS

A cross between a soup and a stew, posole is a classic slow-cooked Mexican dish that combines hominy (alkali-treated dried corn) and chicken or pork. Here, both the Instant Pot® and canned hominy speed up the cooking time.

Season the chicken breasts generously on both sides with salt and pepper. Select Sauté on the Instant Pot® and warm the oil. In batches, sear the chicken until golden brown, about 4 minutes per side. Transfer the chicken to a plate.

Add the onion to the pot and cook, stirring occasionally, until tender and translucent, about 3 minutes. Add the garlic, chile, oregano, cumin, 1 teaspoon salt, and ½ teaspoon pepper and cook, stirring, until fragrant, about 1 minute. Add the hominy and tomatillos and stir to combine. Return the chicken to the pot.

Lock the lid in place and turn the valve to Sealing. Press the Keep Warm/Cancel button to reset the program, then press the Soup button and set the cook time for 20 minutes at high pressure.

Turn the valve to Venting to manually release the steam. When the steam stops, carefully remove the lid and transfer the chicken to a large bowl. Use 2 forks to shred the chicken into bite-size pieces. Return the chicken to the pot, add the lime juice, and stir to mix. Season with salt and pepper.

Ladle into individual bowls. Garnish with the cilantro, avocado, and lime wedges, and serve.

SERVES 6

2 lb boneless, skinless chicken breasts

Kosher salt and freshly ground pepper

2 tablespoons extra-virgin olive oil

1 yellow onion, diced

4 cloves garlic, thinly sliced

1 jalapeño chile, seeded and finely chopped

1 teaspoon dried oregano

1 teaspoon ground cumin

1 can (25 oz) hominy, rinsed

6 tomatillos, husks removed, rinsed, and roughly chopped

Juice of 1 lime

Fresh cilantro leaves, avocado slices, and lime wedges, for garnish

SRIRACHA DEVILED EGGS WITH SPICY BREAD CRUMBS

Vinegary, garlicky Sriracha chile sauce brightens the filling for these easy stuffed eggs. Cooling the eggs in an ice bath after steaming shrinks the egg interior from the shell, making it especially easy to remove.

Pour the water into the Instant Pot® and place the steam rack on the pot bottom. Carefully arrange the eggs on the rack, stacking them on top of one another if necessary. Lock the lid in place and turn the valve to Sealing. Press the Egg button and cook on high, or press the Manual/Pressure button and set the cook time for 8 minutes at high pressure.

While the eggs are cooking, prepare an ice bath. When the eggs are ready, let the steam release naturally for 5 minutes, then turn the valve to Venting to release any residual steam. Carefully remove the lid and transfer the eggs to the ice bath. When the eggs are cool enough to handle, lift them from the water. Crack the egg shells, remove, and discard.

While the eggs are cooling, make the bread crumbs. In a frying pan over medium heat, warm the oil. Add the bread crumbs, garlic, paprika, cayenne, and parsley and cook, stirring constantly, until the crumbs are well toasted, about 3 minutes. Remove from the heat and let cool.

Cut each egg in half lengthwise. Use a spoon to scoop the yolks into a bowl. Set the egg white halves, hollow side up, on a serving platter and set aside. Add the mayonnaise, Sriracha sauce, mustard, and vinegar to the yolks and whisk until no lumps remain. Season with salt and pepper.

Spoon the yolk mixture into a pastry bag fitted with a large star tip and pipe about 1 heaping tablespoon into each egg white half. Top with some bread crumbs and a sprinkle of parsley and serve.

MAKES 24

1 cup water

12 large eggs

½ cup mayonnaise

5 teaspoons Sriracha sauce

2 teaspoons Dijon mustard

1 teaspoon white wine vinegar

Kosher salt and freshly ground pepper

Finely chopped fresh flat-leaf parsley, for garnish

FOR THE BREAD CRUMBS

2 tablespoons olive oil

1½ cups fresh or fine dried bread crumbs

½ teaspoon granulated garlic

½ teaspoon sweet paprika

Pinch of cayenne pepper

2 teaspoons chopped fresh flat-leaf parsley

Pipe the yolk mixture decoratively into the egg white shells, or spoon in the yolks for a simpler approach.

BEEF PITAS WITH RED ONION & TZATZIKI

The popular Greek gyro sandwich has been simplified here with no sacrifice to flavor. Ready all of the sandwich fixings while the beef cooks, including the cool, creamy yogurt-based tzatziki.

Season the beef on both sides with the salt and pepper. Put the beef and onion into the Instant Pot.® In a small bowl, whisk together the water, oil, lemon juice, oregano, and garlic powder, then add to the pot. Lock the lid in place and turn the valve to Sealing. Press the Manual/Pressure Cook button. Set the cook time for 30 minutes at high pressure.

While the beef cooks, make the tzatziki: In a small bowl, whisk together yogurt, cucumber, garlic, dill, and lemon juice. Season to taste with salt and pepper. Set aside until ready to serve.

Let the steam release naturally for about 15 minutes, then turn the valve to Venting to release any residual steam. Remove the lid from the pot and, using a slotted spoon, transfer the beef and onion to a bowl.

To serve, spoon an equal amount of the beef mixture into each pita and top with lettuce, tomato, and onion. Sprinkle with chopped dill and finish with a dollop of tzatziki.

SERVES 8

1½ lb boneless beef chuck, thinly sliced

1 tablespoon kosher salt

Freshly ground pepper

1 yellow onion, thinly sliced

⅓ cup water

3 tablespoons olive oil

Juice of 1 lemon

2 teaspoons dried oregano

1 tablespoon garlic powder

FOR THE TZATZIKI

1 cup plain Greek yogurt

½ cucumber, finely diced

1 clove garlic, minced

2 tablespoons finely chopped fresh dill

Juice of 1 lemon

Kosher salt and freshly ground pepper

8 pita breads

Small lettuce leaves, sliced tomatoes, thinly sliced red onion, and chopped dill for serving

KALE ARTICHOKE DIP

Old-fashioned hot artichoke dip gets an update and a big dose of nutrients with the addition of kale. Assemble this party classic up to a few hours in advance, then slip it under the broiler just before your guests arrive.

Select Sauté on the Instant Pot® and warm the oil. Add the onion and cook, stirring occasionally, until softened, about 3 minutes. Add the garlic and cook, stirring, for 1 minute. Add the artichokes and kale and cook, stirring, until the kale is just wilted and the artichokes have released their liquid, about 7 minutes. Add the cream cheese, mayonnaise, sour cream, ½ cup of the Parmesan, and 1 cup of the mozzarella and stir to combine. The mixture will not be completely smooth; do not overmix. Add the Worcestershire sauce and cayenne, season with salt and pepper, and stir briefly.

Lock the lid in place and turn the valve to Sealing. Press the Keep Warm/Cancel button to reset the program, then press the Manual/Pressure Cook button and set the time for 10 minutes at high pressure. While the dip cooks, set a rack in the upper third of the oven and preheat the broiler.

Let the steam release naturally for 3 minutes, then turn the valve to Venting to release any residual steam. Carefully remove the lid, give the mixture a stir, and transfer it to a broiler-safe baking dish. Top evenly with the remaining ¼ cup each of Parmesan and mozzarella.

Broil until the cheeses are bubbling and lightly browned, about 3 minutes. Serve the hot dip with crostini.

SERVES 6–8

3 tablespoons olive oil

1 yellow onion, finely chopped

2 cloves garlic, minced

1 can (14 oz) artichoke hearts, drained and roughly chopped

1 large bunch kale, stemmed and roughly chopped

1 package (8 oz) cream cheese

½ cup mayonnaise

½ cup sour cream

¾ cup grated Parmesan cheese

1¼ cups shredded mozzarella cheese

1½ teaspoons Worcestershire sauce

½ teaspoon cayenne pepper

Salt and freshly ground black pepper

Crostini or fresh baguette slices, for serving

Long, thin slices of crisp crostini make an efficient tool for scooping up this creamy, cheese-topped dip. Pita or tortilla chips work well too.

TRUFFLE GRUYÈRE MAC & CHEESE

Homey macaroni and cheese is given a touch of dinner-party elegance with a double hit of truffle oil. Go traditional with elbow macaroni, or opt for small shells, cavatappi, campanelle, or other interesting pasta shapes.

In the Instant Pot, combine the macaroni, water, 2 cups of the cream, 4 tablespoons of the butter, and the mustard and season with salt and pepper. Give the mixture a stir, then lock the lid in place and turn the valve to sealing. Press the Manual/Pressure Cook button and set the cook time for 7 minutes at high pressure.

While the macaroni cooks, make the bread crumbs. In a frying pan over medium heat, warm both oils. Add the bread crumbs and parsley, season with salt and pepper, and cook, stirring constantly, until the crumbs are well toasted, about 3 minutes. Remove from the heat.

Turn the valve to Venting to manually release the steam. When the steam stops, carefully remove the lid, add both cheeses, the remaining ¾ cup cream and 2 tablespoons butter, and the truffle oil and stir to mix well.

Divide among individual bowls, top with the bread crumbs, and serve.

SERVES 6–8

1 lb macaroni or any type of short dried pasta

2½ cups water

2¾ cups heavy cream

6 tablespoons unsalted butter

2 teaspoons dry mustard

Kosher salt and freshly ground pepper

1½ cups shredded Gruyère cheese

1½ cups shredded Cheddar cheese

3 tablespoons truffle oil

FOR THE BREAD CRUMBS

2 tablespoons olive oil

2 tablespoons truffle oil

1 cup fresh or fine dried bread crumbs

2 tablespoons chopped fresh flat-leaf parsley

Kosher salt and freshly ground pepper

ONE-POT PASTA WITH TOMATO, BASIL & MOZZARELLA

With the Instant Pot, you can cook the pasta and the sauce together, saving both cooking and cleanup time. Penne has been used here, but garganelli or ziti would also be good.

Select Sauté on the Instant Pot® and warm the oil. Add the onion and cook, stirring occasionally, until translucent, about 3 minutes. Add the garlic, salt, oregano, red pepper flakes, and few grind of black pepper and cook, stirring, until fragrant, about 1 minute. Add the penne, tomatoes, water, and basil and stir to mix.

Lock the lid in place and turn the valve to Sealing. Press the Keep Warm/Cancel button to reset the program, then press the Manual/Pressure Cook button and set the cook time for 5 minutes at high pressure.

Let the steam release naturally for about 15 minutes, then turn the valve to Venting to release any residual steam. Carefully remove the lid, stir in the Parmesan, and season with salt and pepper.

Divide the pasta among individual bowls, top with the mozzarella, garnish with basil, and serve.

SERVES 6

1 tablespoon extra-virgin olive oil

1 yellow onion, thinly sliced

4 cloves garlic, minced

1 tablespoon kosher salt

2 teaspoons dried oregano

1 teaspoon red pepper flakes

Freshly ground black pepper

1 lb dried penne

1 can (28 oz) diced tomatoes with juice

2 cups water

½ cup whole fresh basil leaves, plus more for garnish

¼ cup shredded Parmesan cheese

6 oz fresh mozzarella cheese, shredded

A last-minute addition of shaved Parmesan thickens the risotto to a perfect, creamy consistency.

RISOTTO WITH PANCETTA, PEAS & MUSHROOMS

The Instant Pot® simplifies risotto making by eliminating the need to add the broth in increments and to stir nearly constantly. If you cannot find pea shoots at the market, use tender leaves of baby arugula instead.

Select Sauté on the Instant Pot® and melt the butter. Add the shallot and cook, stirring occasionally, until translucent, about 2 minutes. Add the garlic and thyme and cook, stirring, until fragrant, about 1 minute. Add the rice and stir until it looks slightly translucent and has a nutty aroma, about 3 minutes. Pour in the wine and stir until the wine is reduced by half, about 2 minutes. Add the broth.

Lock the lid in place and turn the valve to Sealing. Press the Keep Warm/Cancel button to reset the program, then press the Manual/Pressure Cook button and set the cook time for 10 minutes at high pressure.

While the rice cooks, in a large sauté pan over medium heat, cook the pancetta, stirring often, until the fat starts to render, about 3 minutes. Add the mushrooms and continue to cook, stirring occasionally, until the mushrooms are tender, about 5 minutes. Stir in the peas and cook until heated through, about 1 minute more. Season with salt and pepper.

Turn the valve to Venting to manually release the steam. When the steam stops, carefully remove the lid and stir in the pancetta-mushroom mixture. Add the Parmesan, stir to mix, and season with salt and pepper.

Spoon onto individual plates or shallow bowls, garnish with pea shoots and Parmesan, and serve.

SERVES 4

¼ cup (60 g) unsalted butter

1 shallot, minced

2 cloves garlic, minced

1 tablespoon fresh thyme leaves

1½ cups Arborio rice

⅔ cup dry white wine

4 cup chicken broth

3 oz pancetta

1 lb mixed fresh mushrooms, such as shiitake, cremini, French horn, and gypsy, brushed clean and thinly sliced

1 cup frozen peas, thawed

Kosher salt and freshly ground pepper

¼ cup shaved Parmesan cheese, plus more for garnish

Pea shoots, for garnish

CHORIZO & SEAFOOD PAELLA

In Spain, paella is classically prepared in a wide, shallow metal pan over an open fire and must be tended nearly constantly as it cooks. The Instant Pot® simplifies the process, cooking quickly and with little effort from the chef.

Select Sauté on the Instant Pot® and warm 2 tablespoons of the oil. Add the chorizo and cook, stirring occasionally, until lightly browned and warmed through, about 4 minutes. Transfer the chorizo to a plate.

Warm the remaining 2 tablespoons oil in the pot. Add the onion and minced garlic and cook, stirring occasionally, until the onion is tender and translucent, about 3 minutes. Season with salt and pepper, then add the smoked paprika, sweet paprika, granulated garlic, and saffron. Cook, stirring often, until the onion is well coated with the spices, about 3 minutes. Pour in the wine and, using a wooden spoon, scrape up any browned bits from the pot bottom. Add the tomatoes, rice, 4 cups of the broth, and the clams, discarding any clams that fail to close to the touch.

Lock the lid in place and turn the valve to Sealing. Press the Keep Warm/Cancel button to reset the program, then press the Manual/Pressure Cook button and set the cook time for 8 minutes at high pressure.

Turn the valve to Venting to manually release the steam. When the steam stops, carefully remove the lid, press the Keep Warm/ Cancel button to reset the program, then select Sauté. Add the remaining ½ cup broth, the shrimp, and the peas and cook, stirring occasionally, until the shrimp are opaque throughout, about 5 minutes.

Divide the paella among individual bowls, discarding any clams that failed to open. Top with parsley and a squeeze of lemon juice and serve.

SERVES 6–8

4 tablespoons olive oil

1 lb cured Spanish chorizo, cut into 1-inch-thick slices

1 yellow onion, diced

3 cloves garlic, minced

Salt and freshly ground pepper

2 teaspoons smoked paprika

1 teaspoon sweet paprika

½ teaspoon granulated garlic

½ teaspoon saffron threads

½ cup dry white wine

1 can (14 oz) crushed tomatoes with juice

2 cups basmati rice

4½ cups chicken broth

1 lb littleneck or other small clams

¾ lb large shrimp, peeled and deveined with tails intact

1½ cups frozen peas

Chopped fresh flat-leaf parsley and lemon wedges, for serving

Studded with thick slices of chorizo and liberally seasoned with two types of paprika and loads of garlic, this Spanish favorite begs for a cold beer or glass of sangria.

BUTTER CHICKEN WITH BROWN RICE

Chicken cooks to perfection in a heady mix of spices and juicy tomatoes. To make this simple preparation a complete meal, add about 2 cups of cut vegetables, such as cauliflower florets or green beans, with the tomatoes.

Select Sauté on the Instant Pot® and melt the ghee. Add the onion and cook, stirring occasionally, until tender and translucent, about 3 minutes. Add the garlic, ginger, chile, cinnamon, garam masala, paprika, coriander, turmeric, salt, and pepper and cook, stirring, until fragrant, about 1 minute more. Add the chicken and cook, stirring occasionally, until cooked through, about 5 minutes. Stir in the tomatoes.

Lock the lid in place and turn the valve to Sealing. Press the Keep Warm/Cancel button to reset the program, then press the Manual/Pressure Cook button and set the cook time for 10 minutes at high pressure.

Turn the valve to Venting to manually release the steam. When the steam stops, carefully remove the lid, stir in the cream, and season with salt and pepper.

Spoon the rice onto individual plates and top with the chicken. Garnish with cilantro and serve.

SERVES 4

2 tablespoons ghee or vegetable oil

1 yellow onion, diced

4 cloves garlic, minced

1-inch piece fresh ginger, peeled and grated

½ jalapeño chile, seeded and minced

1 cinnamon stick

1 teaspoon garam masala

1 teaspoon smoked paprika

1 teaspoon ground coriander

1 teaspoon ground turmeric

1 teaspoon kosher salt

¼ teaspoon freshly ground pepper

2 lb boneless, skinless chicken thighs, cut into 1½-inch cubes

1 can (15 oz) diced tomatoes with juice

½ cup heavy cream or coconut milk

Cooked brown rice, for serving (page 53)

Fresh cilantro sprigs, for garnish

COQ AU VIN BLANC

Here, the famed coq au vin is updated with white wine in place of the traditional red Burgundy and a last-minute addition of cream, mustard, and tarragon. Serve with mashed potatoes and a simple green salad.

Season the chicken thighs on both sides with salt and pepper. Select Sauté on the Instant Pot®and warm the oil. In batches, sear the chicken until browned, about 4 minutes per side. Transfer the chicken to a plate. Add the onion and bacon to the pot and cook, stirring occasionally, until the onion is tender, about 3 minutes. Add the garlic and cook, stirring, until fragrant, about 1 minute. Add the mushrooms and cook, stirring occasionally, until tender, about 5 minutes more. Return the chicken to the pot and pour in the wine.

Lock the lid in place and turn the valve to Sealing. Press the Keep Warm/Cancel button to reset the program, then press the Manual/Pressure Cook button and set the cook time for 10 minutes at high pressure.

Turn the valve to Venting to manually release the steam. When the steam stops, carefully remove the lid and stir in the cream, mustard, and tarragon. Season with salt and pepper.

Transfer the chicken and sauce to a serving platter, top with the pine nuts, and serve.

SERVES 4–6

2 lb boneless, skinless chicken thighs

Kosher salt and freshly ground pepper

2 tablespoons extra-virgin olive oil

1 red onion, diced

¼ lb bacon, diced

3 cloves garlic, minced

2 cups mushrooms, such as maitake or chanterelles, brushed clean and sliced

2 cups dry white wine

½ cup heavy cream

2 tablespoons Dijon mustard

¼ cup lightly packed fresh tarragon leaves, roughly chopped

¼ cup pine nuts, toasted

SESAME–GREEN ONION SHORT RIBS

Korean-style short ribs are those that are cut across the bone, also known as flanken-style—a resourceful preparation that allows them to soak up lots of flavorful marinade and to cook quickly.

To make the marinade, in a blender, combine the soy sauce, sugar, honey, sesame oil, mirin, pears, ginger, garlic, and pepper and process on high speed until well blended, about 30 seconds. Put the short ribs in a large lock-top plastic bag, pour in the marinade, and add the sesame seeds and chopped green onions. Seal the bag closed and shake it gently to coat the ribs evenly. Refrigerate for 24 hours.

When ready to cook, pour the ribs and marinade into the Instant Pot.® Lock the lid in place and turn the valve to Sealing. Press the Manual/Pressure Cook button and set the cook time for 6 minutes at high pressure.

Let the steam release naturally for about 15 minutes, then turn the valve to Venting to release any residual steam. Meanwhile, preheat the broiler.

Carefully remove the lid and transfer the ribs in a single layer to an aluminum foil–lined baking sheet (you may need 2 pans). Place under the broiler until the ribs begin to caramelize and color slightly, about 5 minutes. If desired, press the Keep Warm/Cancel button to reset the program, then press the Sauté button and heat the marinade until reduced by about one-fourth to form a sauce, about 10 minutes.

To serve, arrange the ribs on the rice, then top with the sauce, if using. Garnish with sesame seeds and sliced green onions.

SERVES 4–6

¾ cup soy sauce

¾ cup firmly packed golden brown sugar

¼ cup honey

¼ cup plus 2 tablespoons Asian sesame oil

2 teaspoons mirin

1½ Asian or Bosc pears or gala or honeycrisp apples, cored and roughly diced

2 teaspoons peeled and grated fresh ginger

2 tablespoons grated garlic

1½ teaspoons freshly ground pepper

3 lb Korean-style (flanken-cut) beef short ribs

1 tablespoon sesame seeds, plus more for garnish

6 green onions, coarsely chopped, plus thinly sliced green onions, for garnish

Cooked white rice, for serving (page 53)

A curly green onion garnish makes a lovely presentation. Cut green onions into 2-inch lengths, then cut lengthwise into thin slices. Soak the slices in water until they curl, then drain.

Tomatillo salsa is a zesty addition to pork tamales. Fresh guacamole and tomato salsa are also tasty accompaniments.

PORK & GREEN CHILE TAMALES

Making classic Mexican tamales can be an all-day project. The Instant Pot® cuts the timing in half—streamlining the process by cooking the meat quickly and in the same pot that steams the finished tamales.

Season the pork generously with salt and pepper. Select Sauté on the Instant Pot® and warm the oil. In batches, sear the pork until browned on all sides, about 8 minutes total. Using tongs or a slotted spoon, transfer the pork to a plate. Add the onions to the pot and cook, stirring occasionally, until tender and translucent, about 3 minutes. Stir in the cumin and garlic powder, return the pork to the pot, add the broth and chiles, and give everything a good stir.

Lock the lid in place and turn the valve to Sealing. Press the Keep Warm/Cancel button to reset the program, then press the Manual/Pressure Cook button and set the cook time for 1 hour at high pressure.

Let the steam release naturally for about 10 minutes, then turn the valve to Venting to release any residual steam. Carefully remove the lid and, using a slotted spoon, transfer the pork mixture to a bowl. Using 2 forks, shred the pork. Add the cilantro, season with salt and pepper, stir well and let cool to room temperature. Using pot holders, lift out the inner pot, rinse well, and return the inner pot to the Instant Pot® housing.

Continued on page 46

¾ lb boneless pork shoulder, cut into 4-inch cubes

Kosher salt and freshly ground pepper

2 tablespoons canola oil

1 yellow onion, diced

1 teaspoon *each* ground cumin and garlic powder

½ cup chicken broth

1 can (4 oz) diced green chiles

¼ cup fresh cilantro leaves, finely chopped

Continued from page 45

In a large bowl, mix the corn masa mix, salt, and baking powder, then stir in 3 cups of the water until blended. Stir in the vegetable shortening, then knead the masa against the side of the bowl until incorporated.

Remove the husks from the water and pat dry. Place the husks on a work surface with the narrow ends facing you. One at a time, spread about 3 tablespoons of the masa mixture onto the widest part of a husk and top the masa with about 1 tablespoon of the pork mixture. Fold in the sides of the husk to enclose the filling, then fold up the bottom narrow flap of husk over the center and secure with a narrow strip of the husk. Repeat until all the filling is used.

Pour the remaining 1 cup water into the Instant Pot® and insert the steam rack. Arrange the tamales on the rack, standing them upright. Lock the lid in place and turn the valve to Sealing. Press the Manual/Pressure Cook button and set the cook time for 40 minutes at high pressure.

Let the steam release naturally for about 10 minutes, then turn the valve to Venting to release any residual steam. Carefully remove the lid and transfer the tamales to a plate. Let stand for 15–30 minutes to set up before serving.

MAKES 12–16 TAMALES

4 cups corn masa mix (masa harina for tamales)

2 teaspoons salt

1½ teaspoons baking powder

4 cups water

⅔ cup solid vegetable shortening, melted

16 large corn husks, soaked in water to cover for 1 hour

DULCE DE LECHE RICE PUDDING

The Instant Pot takes all the stirring out of stove-top rice pudding, leaving the cook free to put together the rest of the meal. Use any leftover dulce de leche on your morning pancakes or drizzled over ice cream for dessert.

Combine the rice, dulce de leche, salt, and milk in the Instant Pot, select Sauté, and bring to a boil, stirring occasionally. As soon as the mixture is at a boil, lock the lid in place and turn the valve to Sealing. Press the Keep Warm/Cancel button to reset the program, then press the Rice button.

Meanwhile, in a bowl, whisk together the cream, eggs, sugar, vanilla, and cinnamon.

Let the steam release naturally for 5 minutes, then turn the valve to Venting to release any residual steam. Carefully remove the lid and stir in the egg mixture. Press the Keep Warm/Cancel button to reset the program, then select Sauté and bring the mixture to a gentle boil. The moment it boils, press the Keep Warm/Cancel button until Off appears on the screen.

To serve, spoon the warm pudding into individual bowls and top with whipped cream and a drizzle of dulce de leche, or spoon into bowls, let cool, cover, and refrigerate for up to 2 days, then serve chilled, garnished the same way.

SERVES 8–10

1½ cups Arborio rice

1 cup store-bought dulce de leche, plus more for serving

1 teaspoon kosher salt

5 cups whole milk

1 cup heavy cream

2 large eggs

¼ cup firmly packed golden brown sugar

2 teaspoons vanilla extract

1½ teaspoons ground cinnamon

Unsweetened whipped cream, for serving

CARDAMOM YOGURT WITH ROASTED PEACHES

To make plain Greek-style yogurt for other uses, prepare the yogurt as directed but omit the sugar, cardamom, and other flavorings.

To make the yogurt, pour the milk into the Instant Pot.® Enclose the cardamom pods in a square of cheesecloth and add to the pot. Lock the lid in place and turn the valve to Sealing. Press the Yogurt button until the screen says boil and cook until the milk reaches 180°F, about 25 minutes.

Have ready an ice-water bath. Remove the lid and check the milk temperature with an instant-read thermometer. If it is not 180°F, press the Keep Warm/Cancel program to reset the program, then select Sauté and heat until it reaches 180°F. Remove and discard the cardamom. Transfer the inner pot to the ice-water bath, then stir the milk until it cools to 110°F, about 10 minutes. Transfer 1 cup of the milk to a small bowl, whisk in the yogurt until smooth, then return the milk-yogurt mixture to the pot and add the granulated sugar, cardamom, and vanilla. Whisk until blended.

Return the inner pot to the Instant Pot® housing. Lock the lid in place; the valve can be turned to Sealing or Venting. Press the Keep Warm/Cancel button to reset the program, then press the Yogurt button and set the cook time for 10 hours. When the yogurt is ready (the screen will read Yogt), remove the lid, use pot holders to lift out the inner pot, cover it with plastic wrap, and refrigerate until the yogurt sets, about 4 hours. Do not stir at this point.

When the yogurt is set, line a large fine-mesh sieve with 4 layers of cheesecloth, place the sieve over a bowl, spoon the yogurt into the sieve, and refrigerate for 2 hours to drain.

Meanwhile, prepare the roasted peaches. To serve, spoon the yogurt into individual bowls and top with the peaches.

MAKES 4 CUPS YOGURT; SERVES 6

FOR THE YOGURT

8 cups whole milk

10 green cardamom pods, lightly crushed

2 tablespoons plain yogurt

¼ cup granulated sugar

1 teaspoon ground cardamom

½ teaspoon vanilla extract

Roasted Peaches (page 53)

For regular yogurt instead of Greek, skip the straining step. Whisking the yogurt before serving will make it silky smooth.

Vary the fruit topping if you like, trading out the blueberry preserves and berries for raspberries, strawberries, or blackberries.

BLUEBERRY-PECAN CHEESECAKE

To lower the cake into the Instant Pot® with ease, fold a 20-inch piece of aluminum foil into a 3-inch wide sling and use it to lower the pan into the pot. Leave the sling under the pan, then use it again when the cake is done.

To make the crust, in a food processor, combine the graham crackers, pecans, and brown sugar and pulse to fine crumbs. Add the butter and pulse until combined. Press the mixture onto the bottom of a 7-inch round springform pan. Set aside.

To make the filling, in a stand mixer fitted with the paddle attachment, combine the cream cheese, granulated sugar, and sour cream and beat on medium speed until smooth, about 3 minutes. Stop and scrape down the sides of the bowl. Add the eggs, lemon juice, vanilla extract, and salt and beat on medium-high speed until evenly blended, about 1 minute. Pour the filling into the prepared crust.

Pour the water into the Instant Pot® and insert the steam rack. Using a foil sling (see note), lower the cake pan onto the rack. Tuck the foil ends over the cake, lock the lid in place, and turn the valve to Sealing. Press the Manual/Pressure Cook button and set the cook time for 28 minutes at high pressure.

Let the steam release naturally for 15 minutes, then turn the valve to Venting to release any residual steam. Remove the lid and, using the sling, lift out the cake pan. Let the cake cool, then cover and refrigerate until set, about 2 hours.

About 10 minutes before the cake has set, in a small saucepan over medium-low heat, bring the preserves and lemon zest to a simmer. Add the blueberries and simmer until the berries begin to burst, about 2 minutes. Let cool slightly, then pour the blueberry sauce evenly over the cheesecake. Refrigerate until the topping is set, about 1 hour. To serve, remove the pan sides and cut the cake into wedges.

SERVES 6–8

FOR THE CRUST

2 oz graham crackers

½ cup pecans, toasted

1 tablespoon firmly packed brown sugar

3 tablespoons unsalted butter, melted

FOR THE FILLING

1 lb cream cheese, at room temperature

¾ cup granulated sugar

¼ cup sour cream, at room temperature

2 large eggs, at room temperature

2 teaspoons fresh lemon juice

1 teaspoon vanilla extract

Pinch of kosher salt

2 cups water

½ cup blueberry preserves

1 teaspoon grated lemon zest

1 cup blueberries

CHOCOLATE LAVA CAKE
WITH RASPBERRY SAUCE

If you prefer a less sweet, more intense chocolate flavor for these irresistible cakes, look for chocolate with 60 to 70 percent cacao. For a tangier topping, swap out the whipped cream for whipped crème fraîche.

To make the cake, lightly butter four 4-oz round ramekins, then dust each with about ¾ teaspoon of the sugar. Fill a saucepan about one-fourth full with water and bring to a steady simmer. Combine the butter and chocolate in a heatproof bowl, place over (not touching) the simmering water, and heat, stirring occasionally, until the butter and chocolate melt and are smooth. Remove from the heat, whisk in the sugar, and then whisk in the whole eggs, egg yolks, espresso powder, and vanilla until blended. Sift the flour and salt into the chocolate mixture. Using a rubber spatula, fold in the flour just until no streaks remain. Divide the batter evenly among the prepared ramekins.

Pour the water into the Instant Pot® and insert the steam rack. Place the ramekins on the rack. Lock the lid in place and turn the valve to Sealing. Press the Manual/Pressure Cook button. Set the cook time for 9 minutes at high pressure.

Meanwhile, make the raspberry sauce: In a saucepan over medium-high heat, combine the raspberries and sugar and cook, stirring, until the raspberries begin to break down, about 6 minutes. Add the lemon juice, reduce the heat to low, and simmer until saucelike, about 5 minutes. Strain the mixture through a fine-mesh sieve into a bowl.

When the cakes are ready, turn the valve to Venting to manually release the steam. Carefully remove the lid and let cool slightly, then remove the cakes from the pot. Serve the cakes warm, topped with the whipped cream and the sauce.

SERVES 4

FOR THE CAKE

½ cup unsalted butter, plus more for ramekins

1 cup sugar, plus 1 tablespoon for the ramekins

6 oz semisweet chocolate, roughly chopped

2 large whole eggs plus 2 large egg yolks

1 teaspoon instant espresso powder

1½ teaspoons vanilla extract

6 tablespoons all-purpose flour

¼ teaspoon salt

1 cup water

FOR THE SAUCE

1 package (10 oz) frozen raspberries, or 2 pints fresh raspberries

½ cup granulated sugar

1 tablespoon fresh lemon juice

Whipped cream, for serving

BASIC RECIPES

Cooked Brown Rice

2 cups long-grain brown rice, rinsed

2¼ cups water

Combine the rice and water in the Instant Pot.® Lock the lid in place and turn the valve to Sealing. Press the Manual/Pressure Cook button and set the cook time for 15 minutes at high pressure.

Turn the valve to Venting to perform a quick release. When the steam stops, carefully remove the lid and fluff the rice with a fork. Set the lid on the pot and let sit for 5 minutes before serving.

MAKES ABOUT 4 CUPS

Cooked White Rice

2 cups long-grain white rice

2½ cups water

Combine the rice and water in the Instant Pot.® Lock the lid in place and turn the valve to Sealing. Press the Rice button and set the cook time for 12 minutes at high pressure.

Turn the valve to Venting to perform a quick release. When the steam stops, carefully remove the lid and fluff the rice with a fork. Set the lid on the pot and let sit for 5 minutes before serving.

MAKES ABOUT ABOUT 4 CUPS

Roasted Peaches

6 peaches, halved and pitted

6 tablespoons old-fashioned rolled oats

3 tablespoons unsalted butter, melted

2 tablespoons firmly packed brown sugar

¼ teaspoon ground cardamom

Preheat the oven to 350°F. Butter a 9-inch square baking dish. Arrange the peaches, cut side up, in the prepared dish. In a small bowl, stir together oats, butter, brown sugar, and cardamom, mixing well. Sprinkle the oat mixture evenly over the peaches. Roast in the oven until the peaches are juicy and tender and the topping is browned, 30–35 minutes.

SERVES 6

Steel-Cut Oats

1 cup steel-cut oats

1 cup milk, any kind (dairy, nut, coconut)

2 cups water

Combine the oats, milk, and water in the Instant Pot® and stir to mix well. Lock the lid in place and turn the valve to Sealing. Press the Manual/Pressure button and set the cook time for 10 minutes at high pressure. Let the steam release naturally for about 12 minutes, then turn the valve to Venting to release any residual steam. Carefully remove the lid and serve.

MAKES ABOUT 4 CUPS

Index